The Weather & Our Tempers

poems by

Dominique Townsend

Brooklyn Arts Press · New York

The Weather & Our Tempers
© 2013 Dominique Townsend

ISBN-13: 978-1-936767-11-3

Cover art by Aaron Sing Fox. Design by Joe Pan.

All Rights Reserved. No part of this publication may be reproduced by any means existing or to be developed in the future without written consent by the publisher.

Published in The United States of America by:
Brooklyn Arts Press
154 N 9th St #1
Brooklyn, NY 11249
www.BrooklynArtsPress.com
info@brooklynartspress.com

Distributed to the trade by Small Press Distribution / SPD
www.spdbooks.org

Library of Congress Cataloging-in-Publication Data

Townsend, Dominique.
 [Poems. Selections]
 The weather & our tempers / by Dominique Townsend.
   pages cm
 "Distributed to the trade by Small Press Distribution / SPD"--T.p. verso.
 Poems.
 ISBN 978-1-936767-11-3 (Paperback : alk. paper)
 1. Poetry. 2. Buddhism. I. Title. II. Title: The weather and our tempers.

PS3620.O9584W43 2013
811'.6--dc23

2013004197

10 9 8 7 6 5 4 3 2 1
First Edition

For Aaron & Sage

Contents

to Godavari 11
we would never go to the same place twice, for his restlessness 14
Mikiko at dinner 16
same old shaken bare 18
besieged & embarrassed 23
neti neti 24
things that get passed down 30
to ease what changes 32
a change of name 34
ambition was a bad word 37
irises 38
rhumb 40
three traits 41
causal relations 42
the days go by like so 44
not the memory of an old woman 46
of august birth 50
the weather & our tempers 53
strange bird 54
fear of photos 56
a Brooklyn poem 57
Crane Beach 58
green bicycle 59
lily pads, a gift of the warrior caste 60
long after Paris was made for you 62
to Noah's house 63
verisimilar 66
many years married, he says, 68
these three green feathers 69

about the author

The Weather & Our Tempers

to Godavari

Dry blue dust just after noon,
we searched for the Japanese
place where you recently sat
with a big monk in the rain.

Monsoon's night was too black,
too slick for you to recall the place—
all you knew were salted fish
and kerosene lamps hung out front.

The trouble, you said, started with the king.

It was too hot to walk but we were
always just about there. Flushing
and turned around, you insisted again
we move away from the temple,

only to spot the cracked sign beyond
the clanging of that deaf god's bell.

I ate unremarkably, drank tea
quietly, not wanting to say the place

neighbored my old friend's room
and I noticed his window, open.

We washed hands, gave tips
and agreed on an outing—
to the unblossoming orchids
and fruitless trees of Godavari.

The road was blocked with students.
Dissenting, they sweated and sang toward
their minister's new Garden Of Dreams,
where we'd trespassed on our last date.

Up the hill of the rice green valley, we crouched
where humans might have been sacrificed,
some anthropologist had told you.

The children we smiled at plucked weeds,
walking from school to their ancient dwellings
dangling garlands of countless red chilies.

Near the top our taxi stopped
under a giant gold-faced Buddha.
Through steel gates we played at
demanding to see the orchids.

On the other side a soft-speaking girl moved
too slowly with dry clay-reddened palms and
a handsome man was patient with our climb
down and back, bored by mere green and a dog.

No flowers, as we knew. But our lack
of purpose surprised us more than them,
at ease with nothing ready to buy or sell.

we would never go to the same place twice, for his restlessness

Comfort is to
be at the same
table of the same

café every
day drinking just
one

coffee but
he was
too

restless when
it all started
we were more

like children
making puns
watching late

afternoon
sunlight change
brick

buildings
on Amsterdam by
the cathedral where

we swore
to never go
except as models

for new
angles
I'd offer

him something
real but
we had no

will to go farther
than the corner or
the bookstore.

Mikiko at dinner

Waiting out the monsoon
from an underneath place,
Mikiko hears a mongoose
squawk, spitting its jewels

across a narrow table
of spinach sesame white radish.
She looks older, the child
grown large and complicated.

By the end of the evening
it seems as though she's
telling me to hitchhike
my way around Japan,

shaking off some dream of hers,
but that was twenty years ago.
There was no child and the traveler
was tall and French—a man.

You better take the train, she says.
Later, we walk below banana trees

to her house and to be polite

I ask, *What matters most to you?*

Hot springs in downpours.
Bats at rest. Tall tin pails
of oranges
drum in the rain.

A translation problem—can the din
of petals falling from an orange tree
be deafening? Mikiko laughs it off,
says, *In life one simply needs to eat.*

same old shaken bare

Believe me
or don't:
I don't want
to be "a------ed"

it's not exciting
anymore

(and even seems
it never was)

it looks like
"attracted"
and seems
like "attached"

but, no.

comings and goings
not reneged, yet
degraded at regular

intervals, related in kind
to words like "libel" "inure"
and "for shame! for shame."

a *habitus* is who you are.

fall—the colors are right
the leaves were mostly
shaken early from their limbs
hail and even a rogue

tornado, habituated

a long time ago
in one of the parks
where I grew up
looking

long at buildings and the charming
light all times of day and some nights
taking up the *longue durée*, one kind

one way, one historiography.

I remembered! something
I'd read about praise and blame
a pair among eight mundane
preoccupations—fear of pain
and hope for pleasures

among them, a throng

of screaming neighbors
encourage runners in
a marathon long overdue

this is when the hands of old-time
clocks turn backwards, for once!
for once! and you tease
that only I can think this way,

allowing meditative discipline
to include the ascetic-perverse
or a sensitivity to climate

"it's beautiful out,"
every one
kept saying

there were children
born in cauls, undocumented
and never to save a sailor from
the cruelty of the sea
or a daughter left unmolested
and hawks resting in the low
limbs of trees shaken bare

picture two endless strings of pearls

streams of dreamed up lockets with images
and images in images and a suggestion:

that past is locked in

nostalgically, how hurtful

there's no life in the ginkgo
yellowed and limp
below on the pavement
a shy old man from Shanghai
is gathering berries, good
and smashed alike

we're liable to long for fame
and fear insignificance over

and over, fear gain and crave
loss, confounding and reversing

until one day in May or maybe
November we see—we'd
sooner be shaken bare than go
the same old same old ways again.

besieged & embarrassed

so nearly embraced

the weather here
a family undone

the ghosts if existent
have been hushed

did we share that dream?

shaken beds, not seismic
& unheard of domestics

can we remember
unashamed

can we go back to the visions
of children

someone outside,

the dog or
the weather changing.

neti neti

the other word for

"gasp for air" can also

mean "console"

(we can't see

or say why)

dear god is this about

whose art is to be valued, whose

work will take effect?

neti neti—

"not this, not this"

ancient rite

&

disappointed

"neither this, nor that"

millennia on &

on conducting

rites about which
nothing is known
to make sense
of what is not

in childhood
nothing
is fair the case
inspired
unconscious
lasting oceanic
reliable afraid
imagined

"not so, not so"

we misunderstood is all
& the frame was all
wrong or even gone

there was no context
for orientation our laughing

echoed in a tunnel dreaming
atop a rusty beginningless
tower in a valley afire

a siren reminds
us so young to
stay indoors to
stay asleep

with a shamefaced image
ignoring a smoke signal
sitting Indian-style

still fashioning
our walls in underwater
scenes dressing the self
doctoring as if playacting
our own image

"neti, neti"

(meaning "no")

**

wind moves ivy to
strangle the old oak

meanness rests here
not remembering

the number of rings
a figure after all unknowable

our parents claim
until the tree is cut

its seasons
accumulate in our hands

(the oak is four hundred
years old today)

the one who's left tries to make sense
of her ancestors raging

for shame or sport
the taboo crossed

unabsolved
all these generations

later

a storm of incoherent stories

of passionless even listless
incest

periodically
the characters undergo

a change of name
fundamental incidental

or cosmetic who can say
factually

it is not the oak
but another tree with

no name
no family

the ivy strangles

**

(not so, not so)

something willing or not
something needs

to be offered up
for the sake of the story

we sleep longer
still growing

even

things that get passed down

if this story were set far away
the mornings would be colder
in Brooklyn it's bright not cloudless
but patched with backlit white
so much brilliance all thick and bored
with characters who used to feel
more deeply than saints moved
back and forth the listless layers
three garbled feelings in a row
two boys and a girl too many
changelings a triangulation embedded in
a dream always showing
up so wounded so sparing so simple

who could name this wanton?

written "out of love" small
letters on the line
approaching each other
particles meek beside stern
verbs all the old grammarians

bent low by shame will pass away
by hook or crook they will
not be boxed up

the worst American dreams
a woman awakened in a crate
underground there was earth
and there were nails until she
woke up in bed covered in
sweat desperate for death to come
before she's buried

these are things that get passed down

in the same way
my grandmother was stricken
with a fear of aneurysms and preferred
instead to picture herself hanging
daily from an old jute rope

to ease what changes

what we are

will change we are

the fear of disturbance

of heedlessness of twisted

ways enclaves bound

still to continue

to speak

of pasts and mappings

directionless an honor

to carry what is new

we are simply not

what we were

until at the end

hawks nest mysterious

and another bird

swoops

and trails past the kitchen

and comes to singing

as if this place

were not New York

in a month so dark

of all the trees the sycamore
takes the longest
to leaf
mimics the birch
aglow in winter light

other homes—
this softening haze
is another city

this morning an Indian
fruit seller tall and shawled
against dawn hidden
in white behind a cart
of oranges a slow
awakening in fog

a change of name

all these are signs of life—
red darkening
mums in a mildewed
cup, a pale candle burned
down by a black and vanished
wick, a bed slept poorly
in then made out
of habit

**

we had in common
a long childhood at rest in the back
of a hatchback Peugeot

mine moved me through
torrents of dark East Coast rain
yours up from Mexico

it was summer then for everybody
and we knew what the lines were for

we had in common

a mother who chose names for us

at random or in fear

and made airtight

predictions about the lovers

we'd cling to or let go

**

while the mind

is clear and restful

flawed

configurations

wishful, wistful,

"he used to _____ me"

"I used to _____ him, too, really"

**

I thought nothing
would come of it
one night in a nearby hotel, pretending
we were in Cannes

outside there were local noises, muffled
protesters and the pale crackle of Sunday traffic
you said, I'll gather hibiscus to embellish the bed

while you lie by your imaginary seaside
wear something blue for the hue of your eyes
and don't be afraid for your reputation

ambition was a bad word

still is in some circles
an undue desire to surge above
or through the pretension

not only to move around

as if running for office
but striving like a foil
in some tragedy

extra worldly extra
amicable extra judicious
beyond reason

and attachment
most people cry over loss

a state of being outside

like sleeping in the backyard week
nights in the crisp decay of fall
when stars are a shower of light needles in the black

irises

Since we know now
writing was meant to enslave

the first words
I wrote for you
were from too long ago

when he of
the injured eyes
was the gold
standard make-
believe

I did love
but in agony
we joked of irises
that would
open if only
I would

divert my eyes
too full
of impossible

it all happened
as in a book
I call *The Other*
First Poem
for B—.

rhumb

a straight endless course
for a ship driven by a blind wind

there are rooftops in this town where
dreamers can think over jumping

in this at least they aren't alone

a lot has taken place
that might well have been left out

left to history, the unconscious

idealists are so mean
and romantics so ribald in

response to the pragmatist's wish
to navigate prodigiously by starlight

three traits

still hot at evening the concrete
stings the soles of feet as she
stands smoking, her back turned
in orange cotton from the west.

feed the crows, she suggests
but then—they come so near!
the day before it was not the birds
we fed and feared, remembering.

fifteen years before her soulmate
(in retrospect one can say all words)
hid potatoes from the cook to rot
so he could feed the monkeys
at a temple that hovers behind her house.

no matter where she
moves, on a terrace near sundown,
she shows no age from the back.

these traits of love outlast,
she stands counting back
and forth, in smoke.

causal relations

I hoped to write a poem "After
Akhmatova" like countless women
she was moved by her own
poem tripping down a flight
of stairs her fingers just dusting
the banister wringing her hands
like bells after an argument
her man dead quiet fed up
her jealousies well-founded

or no

outside in Petersburg
for Anna and her lover
it was raining
in Brooklyn there was snow
so cold we hardly knew

the other

I had been in love till
recently you had been
sharing your bed—I suspected

other women pretty and slim
or worse, like me, shared
the red toothbrush you gave me

we're no great Russians

the poem is frail a fort
cardboard and collapsing
somehow a touch like
hers a simple miracle
a man like him fortunate
moustachio'd I think—
beloved of an artist

although
who but a quiet man like that
can translate silence?

he sends her in from the rain
beyond frustration
beyond humor,
beyond patience, knowing

we are at home here

the days go by like so

I can't stop thinking
of the earthquake, small
like the daily almost imagined
ones we used to nod
to each other about
in the valley over dinner.

The days go by like so.
Everybody to her work and
him to his. There are places
where work is to be done
and others are for sleeping.

I once lived with a man
who spent his youth
in a Chinese prison—
no kidding. His days

went by like so: carrying
rusted buckets leaking
from toilet to garden.

The produce was gargantuan.

When his cellmate made it
out to our place for dinner
some twenty odd years later
all they dared talk about
was that epic card game
the one had won
in laughter.

not the memory of an old woman

That last morning

in Paris I took a bath

under a fogged window

in the tub I shared

four summers

before with a lover

and stood barefoot

on the cold kitchen floor

taking it all so

personally.

Later, knowing I could

miss my flight

I walked in meek rain

to a café further

than the usual

thinking

I might reach

the statue we

had laughed about—

a military man

on horseback with his
sword at rest, it seemed,
in the ass of his mount.

Instead I sat
on a wet woven seat
in brief sun
and knew it didn't
shine for me.
I read news
of far away
and drank my coffee
too slowly, the last
of it cold and acrid.

The waiter
was professional,
correct, adult
not quick to turn
like the boys with dark
unkempt curls
in places nearer by.

I'd let the chance to think
of anything pass,
walking back
towards the place
my bags sat packed.

I passed through
the park Jon loved
make-believe
with firsts of spring
forced by some
hired shovel
cheerful
in the fog and mud.

Rounding
a blossomless
green corner
on a scent of sweet nut
I tried to find the summers
passed with that lover
but couldn't quite.

I circled back
broke off one sprig

then another

but as before

the scent was only

in the air.

Locking the door descending

the dark spiral stairs

I decided to carry

my things

with grace and smiled

to think

he used to carry

everything.

# of august birth

all the plants in the studio
reach green for the window
which of them noble?

they need a deeper pot

and the wildflowers
purple phlox yellow
goldenrod Queen Anne's lace
I picked upstate
that weekend while the baby
was still small
dried and scattered

now our mother is in touch

with everyone who's frightening
to us from childhood
who people our dreams
who make us feel bad

one wrong turn of a mood
can draw one to a window
well beyond the pale
to think over words
like hurtle and hurl

(this has roots
in an exchange with
a maternal grandmother)

Dorothy stood by the window
where she ate grapefruit pink and pouring
out the corners of her mouth

over the kitchen sink
where all of us were
bathed as babies

the window where generations
before the sheets of children (shamed
before neighbors) hung out to dry

why else would she wash
them again this week?

where girls scraped their plates clean
and excused themselves to get rid
of dinners and slivers of cake

where numberless wrens nested
and wrecked the brick under an ivy
tapestry on the back of the house

we were all so attached
to the twittering
and the flights

where women too tired would lean
once again watching a man crash down
the steps after slamming the back door

it happened like this
on the back end of summer,
somebody's birthday

the weather & our tempers

yesterday a rainbow bent a corner
over a harbor crammed with sails

today, suggestions of a hurricane

the light in morning
gray and bright
remarkably
failed to still my
mind from needling
through details

of a discordant wake-up

these small failures—
the weather, our tempers

strange bird

the cuckoo is famously odd
but there are others—

the cave swift, sweetest nester,
spits a fine spun sugary paste
a web of twigs
cooked up one day
in a soup for locals

an average gull rides a gust
near Breezy Point intending
to smash a clam

the huge vain loon
if he knows you're interested
will preen like hell
flapping encyclopedic wings
till his pounds become dead weight
and he sinks into the muck
deep and cold beneath his home

the lake

where iris and calla lily go wild
a cuckoo steals into a stranger's nest
leaving another to gather for her young

who will anyway grow up brood parasites
like their mother

and hers before her

fear of photos

She never thought of herself as someone who feared for her soul, never really believed anyone feared photos, suspected some traveler researcher participant observer to have invented this quaint trait for the Beijing con, the uninterested spearman, the woman who hawks blossoms before a temple deflecting anecdotes that suggest she's a kitten in bed between men who say such things in shops over coffees. Then some night replaced and spooked she remembered a strip of photo booth likenesses of her face all in innocence on the edge of a bad fall day with a friend just back from having been estranged. Ruddy and making pretty at the flash, a friend come back, a face bettered by weather and by age that year (however you might look today you'll never look so good again, her mother told her dry and right). All at once she knew fear and if she had a soul her soul could be lost could be lost spirited away tampered with twisted crushed or damaged somehow in the ways a soul or spirit is needled or rented and ruined. So as a matter of course she asked him for the photos back but they'd been thrown away.

a Brooklyn poem

- for Zen master Ryokan, in response to "Reading the Eihei Record"

When I read Ryokan's poems—
who but Buddha knows loneliness so well?

He laid the name
of each town he suffered through
down between lines of wormwood,
starvation, begging bowl, clearheadedness.

Cold in the collapse
of a home made in spring
for acanthus, cosmos, pinks,
chrysanthemums, it was a winter rain

he framed for having ruined all his books,
wept over and over, remembering.

In Brooklyn the comfort is his ease with misery.

Crane Beach

you swatted horseflies
with my sandal
and we noted the inverted
weight of insects where
Buddhists make merit

you surprised me next
with your dauntless generosity
and then again by the width
of your eyes in fearful times

how I manipulated and dabbled
sinking and rising before you
to watch light move
from the water to your skin

the physics of the wave the sun
the salt and us—I treated them as a child
would, playful and deeply testing
the owl charm I wanted from a roadside
hobbyist not interested in profit cost a dime
but having done away with petty change
you had me buy it for myself

green bicycle

By then too much had already been said. The day was not so much stormy as close. A woman rattling on a slow green bicycle (she was elegant in the same soft blouse both yesterday and the day before that) realized as she passed a man on foot, *We're all just here to break each other.* The force of cause and effect is terrific and awful when you understand it. She said this aloud and then to herself or else to the man she said, *This has nothing to do with you!*

lily pads, a gift of the warrior caste

I had shown

that I admired

the water lilies

the old fair

Chhetri lady

drew me

roots and all

from among her

red-gold fishes

now rotting

slowly sinking

soft and yellow

in the hand-hammered

copper bowl

I bargained for

at Asan Tole

the boy whose

family's stall

had sat at that corner

for eleven generations

grinned and touched

my money to his forehead

as I walked on

through the market

though he had wanted

twice what I would give him

I had hopes

that they would last

long after Paris was made for you

Since you wanted to meet the Mona Lisa
I had a sort of fit resting on a bench before
the Pyramid. What the hell's to come of this?
In L'Orangerie and over crêpes we had better luck
just connecting. You fell in love with a Poseidon
fountain thick with algae and sunken terrariums.
We returned to him again and again, glad you
had some taste. The one man you weren't jealous
of I charmed the pants off of. A goose farmer
of all things with fourteen generations and
a wine cart behind him. Later I'd drink his wine
with the man whose garden and pond you tend
and alone one night without a fire I'd eat the
goose's liver. The day we left France we sat
with people who hate their child sneaking
cheese from the market between bits of bread
and water from the café. You said the city was
made for you and I said, Oh good, that's good.
In our attic flat's deep small tub resting up
for a fight we longed to destroy it all. But it
would be years before you'd smash the phone
under fall's fullest moon only to drive out a moment
later to replace it, in case I called you back again.

to Noah's house

there wasn't meant to be so much
time it was midwinter—
bright and cold

we had driven our way up a mountain
toward Sunshine
where my uncle's Japanese friend used to stay

I won't remember what was talked about
because of the lynx I saw while you
turned down the song glancing up for falling rock

we pass the level place
where you and Noah stand watching
capes billowing aged three

past an unthinkable bend
and after the fire- and schoolhouse
you point to where you were born

I tried not to be surprised

at the grandeur of it all—diamond peaks

bared trees and then the sky

in Noah's kitchen we took off our hats

and rested our elbows on a counter

there were fathers and brothers subtle

with however many missing fingers

like a girl I thought of hot chocolate

as Noah steered us through

and ran a finger across the scrawled engraving

he made in the wood of his window frame

the first night he slept in that bed

"this house was bilt in 1985"

I think it read

in his parents' room a wedding

certificate hangs framed—

the ink a faded orange

there are stories about bears

and calculations about how much labor
it takes to keep a wood stove stoked all winter
we pretend to brave the cold again

to uncover what Noah constructed
in his father's studio stacks of small paintings
and all around plans to expand

down the frozen road pale gray rose
from your father's house and yours and others
counting up the antiqued and disappeared

cars that used to rust by that shack
we were quiet about whether
anyone could ever come back

verisimilar

it all appeared real
this round

everything went wrong
we became a stranger

observing us
from a balcony

built by an author
who writes an old man

"un homme
d'un âge"

in his pajamas
in a novel

removed from where
his ideas hold sway

(celebrated)

as if he had nothing
to do with himself

the woman
who visits

his first storey
flat drifts off

tasting of a cooled
clear broth

her thinking
turns by his side

it would be easy to say
he's lived for too long

a woman
"of a certain age"

has a sexual sense
in French—

nothing
is wasted

many years married, he says,

I've looked absentminded
expecting you in doorframes,
daydreamed of you
with a clay pot of yogurt—
the gifts I gave you then.

(You've grown thin and old.)
Instead of a greeting, she coughs.

My wife lives far from here, he says.

Then she see his sleeves and cuffs,
still dusty from some road.

Years later she laughs
to have asked him nothing then
but to say that word (wife)
in a language
she wouldn't understand.

these three green feathers

you ask what bird they fall from

and where are the tiny crying parrots
that used to swoop and trail us
through the neighbor's rice fields

I've seen a man trot through these alleys
balancing two bulbous cages of foreign birds
to be sold and released as gifts to Buddha

the paddies are deep ponds in summer

last night the frogs sang so loud
we yelled across our salad bowls
your back was towards the window

what I didn't tell you: I saw white egrets
pierce the green glistening surface
to feast on these, our favorite musicians

DOMINIQUE TOWNSEND received her BA from Barnard College, a Master's from Harvard, and a PhD from Columbia. She currently teaches Buddhism at Barnard College. She lives in Brooklyn with her family.

Printed by Libri Plureos GmbH in Hamburg, Germany